Beside the Seaside

Poems
By
Barbara Burke Pearce

Beside the Seaside
Copyright 2016
By
Barbara Burke Pearce
In Cooperation with Vision Novels
Printed in the United States of America
All rights reserved.
ISBN: 978-1-941271-13-1

The material in this book, represents the artistic visions of the author published herein and is her sole property, all rights belong to the author. No part of this book may be reproduced, stored in a retrieval system, or transmitted by any means — electronic, mechanical, photocopying, recording, or otherwise — without written permission from the author, except for review purposes.

1. Poetry/American/General
2. Poetry/General

Cover & Interior Art: Kate Pashone
Interior Formatting: Jo Wilkins

614 Mosswood Dr.
Henderson, NV 89015
www.info@visionnovels.com

To Bob –
my everything, my love

We all come from the sea.
But we are not all of the sea.
Those of us who are, we children
of the tides, must return to it
again and again, until the
day we don't come back, leaving
only that which was touched
along the way.

Frosty Hesson

From the movie
Chasing Mavericks

Beside The Seaside

Oh! I do like to be beside the seaside
I do like to be beside the sea!
I do like to stroll along the Prom, Prom, Prom!
Where the brass bands play:
"Tiddely-om-pom-pom!"
So just let me be beside the seaside
I'll be beside myself with glee
And there's lots of girls beside,
I should like to be beside,
Beside the seaside!
Beside the sea!

John A. Glover-Kind
Chorus circa 1907

Table of Contents

A Walk on the Beach
~ 1 ~

The Cottage
~ 3 ~

Destiny
~ 5 ~

Desert Gulls
~ 7 ~

The Sandpiper
~ 9 ~

Monterey
~ 11 ~

A House by the Sea
~ 13 ~

A Seagull's Life
~ 15 ~

Down by the Blue Green Sea
~ 17 ~

A Memory
~ 19 ~

A Seaside Town
~ 21 ~

A Windswept Beach
~ 23 ~

Mermaid
~ 25 ~

Beach Dogs
~ 27 ~

Just You and Me
~ 29 ~

Sea Glass
~ 31 ~

Starfish
~ 33 ~

The Glass Jar
~ 35 ~

Willy
~ 37 ~

Beside the Seaside

A WALK ON THE BEACH

I took a walk on the beach today,
The sky was a foggy swirl of gray.
Seagulls skipped happily down the shore,
Their loud bird cries a steady encore.

Chill ocean spray tap danced on the breeze,
Oh, the wonder of blue windswept seas!
As I walked along with collar high,
The sea, she sang a sweet lullaby,

That lifted my heart and soothed my soul,
It's the missing piece that makes me whole.
Soon the gulls took flight and soared with ease,
Oh, the wonder of blue windswept seas…

THE COTTAGE

There is a cottage by the sea,
Where flowers grow abundantly.
Their colored petals touched by mist,
Beneath the sun they're sweetly kissed.

And fragrant roses scent the air,
A sweet sachet, an essence rare.
Their perfumed spice rides on the breeze,
To rest upon the emerald trees.

Sandpipers run along the shore,
And overhead the seagulls soar.
Upon white sand pink seashells lie,
As ocean breezes softly sigh.

Enchanted as this place does seem,
Is it for real or just a dream?
There is a cottage by the sea,
Where flowers grow abundantly…

DESTINY

His boots kick up a cloud of dust
That fills the desert air.
Her shoes she leaves upon the shore,
Preferring her feet bare.

His cowboy hat is pulled down low
To shade his light brown eyes.
Her hair is blowing in the breeze,
Beneath the tropic skies.

He's never been down by the sea,
Or walked a sandy shore.
She's never seen a mountain range,
With snow it sometimes wore.

A boy and girl so far apart,
Not knowing that somewhere,
They'd find each other, fall in love,
And make a perfect pair.

Their boots kick up a cloud of dust,
That fills the desert air.
Their shoes they leave upon the shore,
Preferring their feet bare…

DESERT GULLS

I saw a flock of seagulls
   In the desert sky,

And I wondered…

Were they lost? Did they cry?

I saw a flock of seagulls
   In the desert sky,

And I wondered…

Did they miss the sea? Like me?

THE SANDPIPER

Run, little sandpiper, run by the sea.
Waves are a'dancing and winds blowing free.
Your little stick legs and countenance grand,
Carry you swiftly o'er seashells and sand.

Run, little sandpiper, run by the sea.
I watch as you pause 'neath a sea grape tree.
I smile as you start your journey once more,
Playing your games with the waves on the shore.

Happy to be in the cool ocean air,
Never a worry and never a care.
Run, little sandpiper, run by the sea.
Oh, how I wish you'd trade places with me…

MONTEREY

I'd rather be in Monterey,
I think I'll pack my bags today.
I'm tired of this desert heat,
It's fresh seafood I want to eat.

To feel the sand between my toes,
And raindrops fall upon my nose,
To hear the seabird's soulful sound,
And count the shells that I have found.

I want to feel the cool sea breeze,
And touch the dew upon the trees.
I'd rather be in Monterey,
I think I'll pack my bags today!

A HOUSE BY THE SEA

When my hair is all gray,
And my body is old,
When the songs are all sung,
And the tales are all told,

Let me live out my days
In a house by the sea,
With the fresh ocean breeze
Blowing softly 'round me.

Let me feel the smooth sand
On my tired old toes.
Let me smell the salt air
With my elderly nose.

Let me gather seashells,
And 'tis happy I'll be.
Let me live out my days,
In a house by the sea…

A SEAGULL'S LIFE

A seagull I would like to be,
To fly so high above the sea,
To rest upon the sandy shore,
And listen to the ocean's roar.

I'd talk to all my seagull friends,
And learn the latest seagull trends,
And as we sat upon the sand,
We'd hear the latest seagull band.

We'd dine on clams and oysters too,
As we enjoyed our ocean view.
Oh, if a seagull I could be,
To fly so high above the sea!

DOWN BY THE BLUE GREEN SEA

I left my footprints in the sand,
Down by the blue green sea.
And as I walked I glanced behind,
And there they followed me.

I walked a mile, maybe two,
The air was crisp and clear.
My footprints pleasant company,
While bringing up the rear.

And so we wandered, not a care,
With seagulls flying o'er.
Their loud cries harmonizing with
The ocean's restless roar.

The sun was setting in the sky,
With colors red and gold.
A pretty scene to tuck away,
Within my heart to hold.

And so the time had come to go,
And when I'm here no more,
Look closely and you just might see
My footprints on the shore…

A MEMORY

I thought I heard a seabird call,
   Though far away is he.
I thought I felt a touch of spray,
   Blown briskly off the sea.

I thought I smelled the salty air,
   And perfumed flowers sweet,
I thought I felt the smooth white sand,
   So soft beneath my feet.

I thought I saw the diamond lights,
   The moon cast on the bay.
I thought I heard the whispering
   Of palm trees as they sway.

I thought I heard a seabird call,
   Though far away is he.
Alas, I realize now that it
   Was just a memory...

A SEASIDE TOWN

There's nothing like a seaside town,
To lift you up when you are down.
Just take a walk 'round narrow streets,
And browse quaint shops for wondrous treats.

Then stop for lunch of tasty fare,
And sit outdoors in salted air,
As weathered boats go sailing by,
And seabirds dance upon the sky.

When walking on a sandy beach,
What treasures lie within one's reach!
Sea glass sparkling like jewels of green,
Or golden amber and citrine.

Mermaid's money and scattered shells,
Painting the shore in soft pastels.
Driftwood sticks all gnarled and brown,
Starfish and urchins all around.

Castles of sand that wash away,
When tide comes in at close of day.
A crab peeks from his hidey hole,
As shorebirds walk their beach patrol.

When harbor lights begin to glow,
Remember, if you're feeling low,
Or when life's trials get you down,
There's nothing like a seaside town…

A WINDSWEPT BEACH

If a windswept beach is within your reach,
You're a lucky soul indeed.
It's the spot to go when you're feeling low,
It's the thinking place you need.

As the wild winds sigh and the seabirds fly,
O'er the whitecaps on the blue,
Let the sea foam spray blow your cares away,
And you'll feel your heart beat true.

It's where dreams can soar the Forevermore,
And your troubles fade away.
It's where peace resides with the ancient tides,
And harmony comes to stay.

Feel your mind explore and your spirits soar,
'Til your worries seem like few.
If a windswept beach is within your reach,
Oh, a lucky soul are you!

MERMAID

I saw a mermaid on the sand,
As waves rolled in to shore.
Her face peeked out from seaweed hair,
A strand of shells she wore.

The gulls and seabirds gathered 'round,
As if to catch a glance.
They lingered for a while, and then
Resumed their hurried dance.

I saw a mermaid on the sand,
As waves rolled in to shore.
But soon the tide came creeping in
And there she lies no more…

BEACH DOGS

I wish all dogs were beach dogs,
If only for a day,
To chase the waves, bark at birds,
And shake the sand away.

Country dogs and city dogs,
Both pedigree and hound,
Great big dogs and tiny dogs,
And sad ones in the pound.

All dogs should know the magic
Of sparkling seaside play.
I wish they all were beach dogs,
If only for a day…

JUST YOU AND ME

Sweet little dog, how did we come to be
At the edge of the world, just you and me?

The wind and the waves and the sky above
With you in my arms…a bundle of love.

Dear little dog, how did we come to be
On a rugged cliff by the churning sea?

In a big wide world, no reason or rhyme
Just you and me…and a moment in time…

SEA GLASS

A bottle fell into the sea,
A long, long time ago.
It tumbled, tossed and rolled about
And soon it sank below.

It traveled with the changing tides
For many, many years,
'Til only shards of glass remained
Like frosted mermaid tears.

In time the pieces washed ashore
And shone upon the sand.
Reflections of the sea and sky
From Mother Nature's hand.

The sea returned to us a gift
All polished and aglow.
A bottle fell into the sea,
A long, long time ago…

STARFISH

I saw a starfish on the shore,
'Twas just the thing for my décor,
Could lean it on my windowsill,
Or place it on a shelf, I will.

Could grace a table in the hall,
Or hang it on my bedroom wall,
Might fasten it into a wreath,
With trailing flowers underneath.

I'd take it home and look around,
Until the perfect spot was found,
Near silent seabirds carved from wood,
Or shells saved from my childhood.

But when I took it from the sand,
And felt it soft against my hand,
I smiled upon this thing so free,
And tossed it back into the sea…

THE GLASS JAR

She keeps her seashells in a jar,
Upon the window sill,
And sometimes when the days grow long,
Or when the nights lie still,

She reaches for the old glass jar,
And handles it with care,
For mixed among the pretty shells,
Are happy memories there.

She spreads them out upon the floor,
Each one a treasured prize.
She sorts and rearranges them,
And lines them up by size.

She smiles as she chooses one,
And holds it to her ear.
She hears the waves lap on the shore,
And seabirds flying near.

She feels the sand beneath her feet,
The warm sun on her face,
And suddenly she's held with love,
In yesterday's embrace.

Now sometimes when the days grow long,
Or when the nights lie still,
She reaches for the old glass jar,
Upon the windowsill…

WILLY

There once was a turtle named Willy,
Who lived on a hill by the sea.
He loved to look out at the ocean,
'Twas nowhere that he'd rather be.

The blue dolphins waved while swimming by,
The whales sang a sweet serenade.
Pelicans sky danced high overhead,
As though in an airborne parade.

There once was a turtle named Willy,
Who lived by the sea on a hill.
He loved when the sun shimmered brightly,
And foggy gray days touched with chill.

There once was a turtle named Willy,
'Twas nowhere that he'd rather be,
Sea spray on his face, joy in his heart,
Perched there on a hill by the sea.

Artist

During the last twenty years **Kathy Pashone** has created art that has been displayed in galleries, painted on rancher's old milk cans, floral designs on benches to murals on walls downtown.

While displaying her artwork in Cayucos, a small town on the Central Coast of California, it captured the eye of poet Barbara Pearce, beginning their creative journey in 2013.

Her art is now displayed in her garden gallery at her home.

"Art is my gift to you, Enjoy!"
Kate Pashone

www.ingramcontent.com/pod-product-compliance
Lightning Source LLC
Chambersburg PA
CBHW042234090526
44588CB00005B/77